United States Presidents

Dwight D. Eisenhower

Paul Joseph
ABDO Publishing Company

visit us at
www.abdopub.com

Published by Abdo Publishing Company 4940 Viking Drive, Edina, Minnesota 55435.
Copyright © 1999 by Abdo Consulting Group, Inc. International copyrights reserved in
all countries. No part of this book may be reproduced in any form without written
permission from the publisher.

Printed in the United States.

Cover and Interior Photo credits: Peter Arnold, Inc., SuperStock, Archive, Corbis-
Bettmann

Edited by Lori Kinstad Pupeza
Contributing editor: Brooke Henderson

Library of Congress Cataloging-in-Publication Data

Joseph, Paul, 1970-
    Dwight D. Eisenhower / Paul Joseph.
    p. cm. -- (United States presidents)
    Includes index.
    Summary: A biography of the World War II general who became the thirty-
fourth president of the United States in 1952.
    ISBN 1-56239-744-3
    1. Eisenhower, Dwight D. (Dwight David), 1890-1969--Juvenile literature. 2.
Presidents--United States--Biography--Juvenile literature. [1. Eisenhower,
Dwight D. (Dwight David), 1890-1969. 2. presidents.] I. Title. II. Series:
United States presidents (Edina, Minn.)
E836.J67   1998
973.921'092--dc21
[B]
                                     97-48301
                                     CIP
                                     AC

Contents

President Eisenhower

*I*n March 1952, President Harry Truman announced that he would not run for **re-election**. The **Republicans** decided to choose a war hero to run for president. That man was General Dwight David Eisenhower.

During World War II, General Eisenhower became one of the most successful commanders in history. After the war was over, he continued on in the **military** as the Army Chief of Staff. Later, he became the first head of the North Atlantic Treaty Organization (NATO).

In 1952, Eisenhower turned to **politics** and was just as successful as he had been in the military. After the Republicans chose him to run for president, Eisenhower easily beat the **Democrats**' Adlai Stevenson. When he took office in January 1953, he became the 34th president of the United States and the first Republican president in 20 years.

Eisenhower was always well liked by Americans. But when he was president, Eisenhower became even more popular. Eisenhower was an honorable man, with an easy-going

President Dwight
D. Eisenhower

personality, and a cheerful grin. "I Like Ike" buttons were worn throughout the United States. "Ike" was a nickname given to President Eisenhower.

Americans also liked Ike because of the way he ran the country. He met with world leaders to make peace. U.S. businesses did well, and most Americans had a job thanks to Eisenhower's ideas.

Eisenhower had to work very hard to become one of the greatest men in American history. It all started in a small town in Kansas.

Opposite page: Eisenhower was admired for his dream of world peace.

Dwight D. Eisenhower (1890-1969)
34th President

BORN:	October 14, 1890
PLACE OF BIRTH:	Denison, Texas
ANCESTRY:	Swiss-German
FATHER:	David Jacob Eisenhower (1863-1942)
MOTHER:	Ida Elizabeth Stover Eisenhower (1862-1946)
WIFE:	Mamie Geneva Doud (1896-1979)
CHILDREN:	Two boys
EDUCATION:	Abilene High School, Kansas (1909); U.S. Military Academy (West Point, New York), graduated 1915
RELIGION:	Presbyterian
OCCUPATION:	Soldier; President of Columbia University (1948-1951)
POLITICAL PARTY:	Republican

MILITARY SERVICE: Commissioned Second Lieutenant in U.S. Army (1915); served in various posts in U.S., Panama, and Philippines (1915-1942); named Commander of European Theater of Operations (1942); named Supreme Commander of Allied Expeditionary Force in Western Europe (1943); promoted to General of Army (1944); named Army Chief of Staff (1945); appointed Supreme Commander of Allied powers in Europe (1951)

OFFICES HELD: None

AGE AT INAUGURATION: 62

TERMS SERVED: Two (1953-1957) (1957-1961)

VICE PRESIDENT: Richard M. Nixon (both terms)

DIED: March 28, 1969, Walter Reed Hospital, Washington, D.C., age 78

CAUSE OF DEATH: Heart Failure

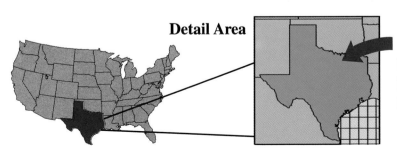

Detail Area

Denison, Texas

Birthplace of Dwight D. Eisenhower

Growing Up in Kansas

*E*isenhower's parents, David and Ida, were married in 1885 in Kansas. A few years later, David moved his family to Denison, Texas. On October 14, 1890, Dwight D. Eisenhower was born.

Eisenhower's given birth name was David Dwight Eisenhower. However, he went by Dwight so he wouldn't be confused with his father. Later in life, Eisenhower changed his name to Dwight David.

The Eisenhowers returned to Kansas when young Dwight was two years old. The future president grew up in the town of Abilene and lived in the house his grandfather had built. The Eisenhowers had a large family with all sons. There was Dwight, Arthur, Edgar, Roy, Earl, and Milton.

In elementary and high school, young Dwight was called "Ike" by his friends. The nickname stayed with him his whole life. In school, Ike was a good student who did well in English, history, and geometry. He was a friendly person, and a good athlete. In high school, Ike starred in both basketball and football.

Ike graduated from Abilene High School in 1909. Ike put his plans on hold for the next two years and worked to help his family. He gave most of the money he made to his brother Edgar so he could attend college.

Ike decided to go to a **military** school. In 1911, he entered the Military Academy at West Point. Ike played on the academy football team. He was an excellent player but he had to quit after hurting his knee. Ike worked hard in the military and graduated in 1915.

Though he finished in the middle of his class ranking, Ike would become one of the greatest men in U.S. military history.

Eisenhower practicing his football kick at West Point in 1912

Mamie and the Military

*E*isenhower's first **military** assignment was in Sam Houston, Texas. On a weekend off from the army, he went to nearby San Antonio. There he met Mary "Mamie" Doud.

Ike and Mamie began dating. On July 1, 1916, the two were married. On that same day, Eisenhower was promoted to first **lieutenant**. Ike was making a name for himself.

In 1917, the Eisenhowers had a son, Doud Dwight. But he died from an illness when he was only three. In 1922, they had a second son, John, who would later have a military career. Army life was hard on the family. Ike was often in other parts of the world. He didn't get to see his family as much as he wanted to.

Eisenhower quickly moved up the ranks. During the war, Eisenhower received ranks of **major** and then lieutenant **colonel**. For his great work in the first world war, Ike received the Distinguished Service Medal—the army's highest award.

Ike and his family lived all over the world while he worked in the military. Eisenhower had assignments in many parts of the United States, the Panama Canal Zone, and in many parts of Europe. In all, the Eisenhowers moved about 28 times.

Because of Ike's great ability to lead, he earned a high post in Washington, D.C., from 1929 to 1933. Eisenhower became General Douglas MacArthur's assistant in 1933. In 1936, Ike was promoted to **lieutenant colonel**. Around that time he learned to fly.

Eisenhower continued to do very well in the army. He received more promotions and awards. It wasn't until World War II that Ike truly became a war hero and a famous name.

Dwight and Mamie Eisenhower after their wedding in 1916

World War II

World War II brought Eisenhower back to the United States. Early on, he was a big part of the United States' success in the war. In 1941, he was promoted to **colonel** and **brigadier general**. The next year, he moved up to **major general** and **lieutenant general**.

In July 1942, Ike was in charge of the **invasion** of North Africa. In this role, he showed great leadership for solving both **military** and **political** problems. The attack on North Africa was successful. Ike soon was promoted to a four-star general.

In 1943, Eisenhower was named the Supreme Commander. He began preparing for Operation Overlord. This was the code name for the invasion of Normandy, France. It would help put an end to World War II. On June 6, 1944, Eisenhower's troops landed in Normandy. The operation made the Germans retreat to Germany. They finally surrendered in May 1945.

Eisenhower's operation was not only successful, but it was also one of the greatest operations in military history. On December 20, 1944, Eisenhower was given the highest military rank. He was named a five-star general of the army.

In 1945, Ike became the head of the entire army when he was named the Army Chief of Staff. In 1948, after one of the greatest **military** careers, Ike retired. That same year Eisenhower became the president of Columbia University. He also wrote a best-selling book about his World War II experience. The book was titled, *Crusade in Europe*.

General Eisenhower (R) with France's General Charles De Gaulle in 1944

The Making of the 34th United States President

1890 Born October 14 in Denison, Texas

1891 Moves to Abilene, Kansas

1909 Dwight, nicknamed "Ike," graduates from Abilene High School

1911 Enters the U.S. Military Academy at West Point, NY

1929 Moves to Washington, D.C., for executive post

1936 Promoted to lieutenant colonel

1942 Appointed major general; takes over planning for invasion of North Africa

1944 Eisenhower receives the highest American military rank—five-star general

1952 Elected 34th president of the United States

1953 Signs truce to end the Korean War

1955 President Eisenhower suffers a heart attack

1956 Re-elected to second term

PRESIDENTIAL

Dwight D. Eisenhower

"The quest for peace is the statesman's most exacting duty...
practical progress to lasting peace is his fondest hope"

1915
Graduates from West Point

1916
Marries Mamie Doud on July 1

1917
First son, Doud Dwight is born; Ike is promoted to captain

Historical Highlights
during Eisenhower Administration

★ Supreme Court declares racial segregation in public schools unconstitutional (1954)

★ Polio vaccine is discovered (1955)

★ NASA is established (1958)

★ Alaska and Hawaii become states (1959)

1945
Becomes Army Chief of Staff

1948
Becomes president of Columbia University in New York City

1957
Eisenhower Doctrine passed; Civil Rights Act signed

1961
Finishes his second term; JFK is elected president

1963
In retirement, writes first of three books

1969
Dies of heart failure on March 28

YEARS

Working for His Country

*A*lthough Ike retired from the **military**, he never stopped working for his country. In 1950, President Truman requested his help in starting NATO. He left Columbia University to once again help his country. NATO is an organization of many different countries that help maintain peace around the world.

Ike's work and success in NATO made him even more popular throughout the country and the world. Eisenhower was very well liked. Americans thought that he would make a great president.

Both political parties approached him about running for president. Eisenhower was honored, but most of all he believed it was a call of duty.

Early in 1952, Ike chose to run as a **Republican**. Republican leaders were very happy. People around the country wanted Ike as their president. On June 4, 1952, Eisenhower officially entered the presidential race with a speech in his hometown of Abilene, Kansas.

Eisenhower was a great **campaigner**. People liked his honesty, hard work, warm personality, and great speaking skills. At the **Republican** meeting in Chicago, Ike was chosen to run for president. **Senator** Richard Nixon, from California, was chosen to run for vice president.

Ike promised Americans that he would work for world peace. To end the Korean War, Ike promised: "I shall go to Korea."

Eisenhower's leadership and great charm brought the country together. Ike would have no trouble winning the next **election**.

General Eisenhower (R) worked very well with the Commander-in-Chief, President Truman.

The 34th President

*O*n November 4, 1952, Dwight D. Eisenhower was **elected** the 34th president of the United States. He received nearly 34 million votes—the most ever by a presidential **candidate** at that time.

Four weeks after his victory, Eisenhower kept his promise and made a trip to Korea. He visited the battlefields of Korea and worked for a peaceful settlement. On July 27, 1953, a peace agreement ended the Korean War.

President Eisenhower took office on January 20, 1953. During his first four years as president, many things happened. Ike chose the second woman in history to be in his **cabinet**. On May 17, 1954, the **Supreme Court** ruled that **races** could not be separated in public schools.

President Eisenhower also chose two new Supreme Court judges. **Congress** outlawed the **Communist** party in the United States. It also raised the least amount a worker could make from 75 cents to $1.00 an hour.

Eisenhower's inauguration in 1953

An important event happened on April 12, 1955. Dr. Jonas E. Salk of Pittsburgh discovered a new drug to stop polio. Polio is a disease that had left thousands of people, mostly children, **paralyzed**. President Eisenhower and the secretary of health came up with a plan to give the new drug to Americans. Today, polio has almost been erased in the U.S.

On September 24, 1955, President Eisenhower and the whole country suffered a scare. Ike was on vacation in Colorado. After a long day of golf, he suffered a heart attack and was rushed to the hospital.

In December 1955, Eisenhower was ready to return to work. Many Americans wondered if he would run again for president in 1956. Ike wanted to show the country that he was healthy enough to be president. He told the nation he would run for **re-election**.

President Eisenhower delivers a speech from the White House in 1955.

Ike Is Re-elected

*A*mericans were glad to see Eisenhower back in office and in good health. The popular president was easily **re-elected** in November 1956. But Ike faced serious problems around the world and at home. People around the world were worried about the spread of **communism**. Ike asked **Congress** for money to help any nation that wanted to fight communism. Congress agreed with Ike and voted for this plan in March 1957. It became known as the Eisenhower Doctrine.

In America, there were problems in the South between white and black people. Southerners wanted separate schools for whites and blacks, and separate water fountains and restaurants. They also wanted African Americans to sit in the back of buses. Black people were not allowed to vote.

It was a very ugly time in American history. Riots and peaceful protests were going on throughout the country. In 1957, Eisenhower signed a Civil Rights Act. This act formed a group that would see why African Americans were treated like second-class citizens in the South. New laws were passed that would give African Americans every right that other Americans had.

President Eisenhower asked **Congress** to create a space agency for research and exploring the universe. Congress said yes to Ike's plan. The new National Aeronautics and Space Administration (NASA) had been formed.

President Eisenhower signed a bill in 1958 that granted Alaska statehood. Alaska officially became the 49th state on January 3, 1959. A few months later, Ike signed a bill that granted the Hawaiian Islands statehood. On August 21, 1959, Hawaii officially became the 50th state.

President Eisenhower meeting with Civil Rights leaders

Ike Goes Home

A new law said that no one could be president more than two times in a row. So, Dwight D. Eisenhower became the first president required by this new law to leave the White House.

January 20, 1961, was Ike's last day as president. Eisenhower moved to his farm in Gettysburg, Pennsylvania, and began raising animals. He also played golf, spent time with his family, and wrote three books.

In March 1968, Ike was taken to a hospital because of poor health. After being in the hospital for over a year, Ike died of heart failure on March 28, 1969.

The **military** hero and president was honored with a three-day funeral service. It drew world leaders, and every-day citizens who loved and respected him.

At the time of his death, Eisenhower's former vice president, Richard Nixon, was president. Nixon spoke at Ike's funeral and revealed to America some of Eisenhower's last words: "I've always loved my wife. I've always loved my children. I've always loved my grandchildren. I've always loved my country."

After the funeral, Eisenhower was buried in his hometown of Abilene, Kansas, in the chapel at the Eisenhower Center. In 1971, Ike became the first president to have his image placed on a dollar coin.

The Eisenhower family celebrates their last Christmas at the White House in 1960.

Fun Facts

•President Eisenhower was the first president to appear on color television.

•Eisenhower became the first president to celebrate his 70th birthday in the White House.

•President Eisenhower was the only president to hold a pilot's license.

•While retired, President Eisenhower scored a hole-in-one while playing golf in Palm Springs, California.

•Eisenhower was the first president of all 50 states. On January 3, 1959, Alaska became the 49th state. And on August 21, 1959, Hawaii became the 50th state. Ike was the president at the time.

•Eisenhower was a great football player in the **military** academy. However, he quit after hurting his knee trying to tackle football legend Jim Thorpe.

Opposite page: Dwight Eisenhower, Supreme Commander of the western armies, 1945

Glossary

Brigadier General—a one-star general.

Cabinet—a person appointed by the president of the United States to work in his administration.

Campaign—to give speeches and tell people your ideas so they will vote you into an elected office.

Colonel—a military rank above major and below general.

Communists—people who practice the type of government known as Communism. This is where every person is the same and people get things based on need.

Congress—a group of elected officials in Washington, D.C., who represent different parts of the United States, and who make laws for the country.

Democrat—one of the two main political parties in the United States. Democrats are known to be more liberal and believe in more government.

Election—a process where people can vote for a public official.

General—the highest military rank.

Invasion—entering by force or as an enemy.

Lieutenant—a military rank above sergeant and below captain.

Major—a military rank above captain and below colonel.

Military—working within the armed forces, such as the army or navy.

Paralyze—to make powerless or helpless.

Politics—being involved in government such as an elected official that makes laws for the city, county, state, or country.

Race—a group of persons having the same ancestors.

Republican—one of two main political parties in the United States. Republicans are known to be more conservative and believe in less government.

Senator—one of two elected officials from a state who represents the state in Washington, D.C. There they make laws and are part of Congress.

Supreme Court—the highest court in the U.S.

Internet Sites

United States Presidents Information Page
http://we.got.net/docent/soquel/prez.htm
Links to information about United States presidents. This site is very informative, with biographies on every president as well as speeches and debates, and other links.

The Presidents of the United States of America
http://www.whitehouse.gov/WH/glimpse/presidents/html/presidents.html
This site is from the White House. With an introduction from President Bill Clinton and biographies that include each presidents inaugural address, this site is excellent. Get information on White House history, art in the White House, first ladies, first families, and much more.

POTUS—Presidents of the United States
http://www.ipl.org/ref/POTUS/
In this resource you will find background information, election results, cabinet members, presidency highlights, and some odd facts on each of the presidents. Links to biographies, historical documents, audio and video files, and other presidential sites are also included to enrich this site.

These sites are subject to change. Go to your favorite search engine and type in United States presidents for more sites.

Pass It On

   History Enthusiasts: educate readers around the country by passing on information you've learned about presidents or other important people who've changed history. Share your little-known facts and interesting stories. We want to hear from you!

To get posted on the ABDO Publishing Company Web site, E-mail us at "History@abdopub.com"
Visit the ABDO Publishing Company Web site at www.abdopub.com

Index